Tabernacle

to Ann Tryon Nicol,
   fellow, lover of Maine.
Enjoy!

       Sam King
       January 2002

Tabernacle

POEMS OF AN ISLAND

SUSAN DEBORAH KING

Susan Deborah King

ISLAND INSTITUTE

Tabernacle: Poems of an Island
© 2001 by Susan Deborah King

Published by
Island Institute
P.O. Box 648
386 Main St.
Rockland, Me. 04841

Cover art titled "Purple Island" ©2001 by Edna Andrade
Cover design by Alicia Velasquez, Mori Studio
Book design and typesetting by Liz Tufte, Folio Bookworks
Author photo ©2001 by Sara Stout

The author wishes to thank the editors of the publications in which
these poems first appeared: "Popplestones," "Jan's Garden," "Tea
Ceremony, Under Apple Tree, August," *The Connecticut Review;*
"Island Lights," "Paying Homage"*: Zone 3;* "Grief's Progress," *Hudson
Valley Echoes;* "Edna's Studio," "Night Vision," "Sally's Oboe," *Arts
Magazine* of United Theological Seminary; "Blueberries," *The Island
Journal;* "Lobelia," "Slug," *The Maine Times.*

ISBN: 0-942719-29-8

Printed in the U.S.A.

This book is dedicated with love

to my family: Jim, Emily, and Enid,

to Virginia D. Murray,

and

to the island and its people

CONTENTS

ACKNOWLEDGMENTS

I wish to thank Brendan Galvin for the inspiration of his example and for help with shaping this manuscript. Special thanks too to Polly Brody for her friendship and critical help and to other Wood Thrush Poets for their nurture and guidance: Patricia Fargnoli, Morgan Finn, Pit Pinegar, Geri Radacsi, Carole Stasiowski, and Jean Tupper. Thanks to teachers Walter Wink, Luella Sibbald and Sheila Moon for their early encouragement and for the steadfast support of friends Renita Sheesley Banks, Reed Banks, Linda J. Clark, Jolinda Osborne, Deirdre Taylor Johnson, Sally Schwager, Bill and Beverly Gaventa, Rhayma Blake, Kathryn Stulla Mackensen, Peggy Mann Rinehart, Alan and Sharon Hulbert, Doris White, Lola Merritt, Charles Kinney, Kathy Callahan, Lynn and Colin Harrison, Ann Chapman, Chris Morrow, Peter and Nadine Oundjian, Ann and Clem Malin, David and Cheryl Purvis, Betty Hill, Lisa Paulson, Ed and Peggy Sanford, Ron and Sue Knape, Judy Horrigan, Susan Ragland, Joanna Hurley, Rosalyn Dischiavo, Eileen Harrington, Claire Willis, Paige Gillies, Joan Poritsky, Donna Calacone, Jayson Engquist and David Winkworth, Lake Dziengel, Julie Neraas, Susan Allen Toth, Pamela Hill Nettleton, Itti Furlong and Susan Stuart Otto. Many thanks to numerous friends at Plymouth Congregational Church in Minneapolis and to all residents of Great Cranberry Island, Maine, for their gift of friendship and community. And deep gratitude to Liz Tufte for the design of this book.

LOBELIA

Spilling from pots and hanging baskets
on porches by doors on this island,
shocks of blue sharper than
swells of ocean greet you:
Hello, hail, heal, health, whole, holy.
These wee, deep blue eyes of God
burn through to your heart
making it *sacré coeur*
and you go away glowing,
a votive flame to today in your chest.

BUOY BELL

This angelus, rung by wave and wind, a warning friend, implores
me: Hearken to dreams, enflesh them and ring with this time.

Hearing it sunny mornings pinning gowns and jeans to the line,
I could strip to the skin and array myself in no more

than dew, wind and light. At night it tolls down my corridor
to the door a man sometimes unlatches, parting me, blinding

us with barrens ablaze with fireweed. And when I walk to shore,
it beckons from the swells to other reaches, other tongues I've

longed to sail beyond this shelf and find. But I cling instead to the inside
world with the door cracked, so the bell peals as I slice from the core

the blood-edged moons of this peach, my head bowed, seeking the force
that can split from this pith a tree, or chime

me like an angelus, rung by wave and wind, a warning friend imploring:
Hearken to dreams, enflesh them, and ring with this time.

PAYING HOMAGE

any August, Cranberry Isles

Up here,
when the sky is clear as it was the first day
and vetch raises purple slubs on
the homespun throw of the field,
when waves range across the Western Way
like azure herds and even trunks of
evergreens are anointed with sun,
when gulls stitch the hours together
with their dips and "yuks" and the
rattling air warns that our time
is almost up and never enough, never enough,
it feels as though the great Whatever-It-Is
has come to call and
I have to drop everything –
books, pots, the vacuum, the phone
and go out to meet it. But with what?
How can I ever be an adequate host?

I burn words onto a page
that go up as nothing but smoke
and bow to the breeze that freshens my sheets,
folding them slow and solemn as altar cloths.
Down an aisle lined with spruces,
over the plush pile of their needles
with their incense cleansing my lungs,
I reach the cove and give up
trying for an in-kind response,
confessing that I'm unequal to
this horizon, undulant with mountains,

blushing hard in yet another shade of love,
and I'm finally still enough to hear
the slup, slup of the tide
rising against the rocks.
I sit on one, giving thanks for the
huge, smooth speckled pink egg of it
that holds me up, and
brood over the changing face of the waters.

GATHERING STONES
IN PREBLE COVE

These scambled fragments draw me
by shape, color or design as if
they were mine or meant for me,
as if they were things I'd lost
sent back by someone from the deep,
whose signature is scraped and marled on this rock
and cannot be made out except
to feel its pitted peaks and cloughs, someone
who knows what all, what more
than I had thought, could live,
could live in me.
Out of this cobbled mass, one will suddenly
zoom in clear and press me
to pick it up and own it,
to read it like a code, and, with wind
and wave brooding over them like eggs,
they crack and breathe in my hands, inside me:
the probe I've lacked to delve with,
a gold and sleek three-sided arrow,
pointing toward a mapstone embossed
with a coast of coral along a charcoal gulf.
This is the terrain where I can claim
in my face the features traced and sculpted
by the tide in other stones I find:
the slant and deep-grooved brow of sorrow;
greed's lewd and drooling lips,
its sallow nose, the leering lids; the wide,
abyssal mouth of need; cheeks piqued to
a flush; pride's jagged, jutting chin.
Mine as well, the pocked, pink chunk
choked with agate claws, too,
the bound and binding energy released
in rust petals from a green globe.

And though a three-eyed beast with
snapping tails, a mouth and torsoful of teeth
roams the wide, white wastes
and gouged-out gorges of these stony spots
and I pine for what lies behind
a cracked, celadon wall,
multifarious rings engrave more stones
than any other theme, assurance
that something at the core is
whole and holding, waiting only for
me with these parts I've gathered
to piece together the broken heart of God.

TEA CEREMONY,
UNDER APPLE TREE, AUGUST

. . . the utmost beatitude of the mundane
— Okakura Kakuzo

A long orange extension cord makes heat
under the kettle possible on this Maine island lawn.
Throw rugs serve as mats.

Since our culture does not have a ritual for
bringing the moment into focus, for
celebrating the golden air of this afternoon,
we three from the Occident, two guided by a *sensei,*
fumble through these foreign procedures
to satisfy our thirst.

Here in the shade, wind drops apples into our laps,
making us laugh at what disruption can add to
the process: hard yellow periods in
the middle of sentences.

Sweets from a pottery jar, whose black glaze
seems to boil with the presence of death,
tumble into our palms – frosty sugar crystals
shaped like hydrangea blossoms:
lavender, pale pink.
We pop them into our mouths and
taste summer melting on our tongues.
There are different versions for every season.
Tomorrow we'll practice autumn,
at night, in a boat,
with a white tea board that reflects the moon.

In a round black lacquer reliquary
with a gilded lid is a powder,
bright chartreuse as the lichen on
boulders at the top of Cadillac, mountain
watching over our shoulders from the mainland.

It is scooped into a bowl – *chawan* –
with a narrow implement that
has been inched out of its silken case –
chashaku – like a snake from its skin.
The tea, mixed with water, is whisked into a foam
with a piece of many-pronged bamboo
that apes the stamens
in the centers of poppies nodding from
a nearby garden.

Offered with both hands, the *cha*
is bitter as the awareness of time passing.
Our eyes dance with each other as
the waning light dances on the ocean beyond us,

and we turn our attention to how
the silk napkin is folded, how the utensils
are wiped clean, how the wrist is turned when
putting the tea back into its brocade bag,
how it is set into the bowl and then into
another bag with purple cords that
knot and unknot as easily as waves.

When everything is carefully placed
into the box used for *chabako*,
this "picnic" kind of tea,
we rock off our knees and
bow to the browning grass.

BLUEBERRIES

They're bluer than the sky, much bluer,
bluer too than this ocean
heaving clefts to crests,
bluer than the cornflower
or the bunting, or the blue
the tremble of music
can bloom inside us;
blue only as the shadow
plumbing the grave into which
this summer so swiftly passes,
or as the deep abiding blue
of lapis, consolation of queens,
these spheres clustering coyly
in shrubs that spread their reddish
green fire over this heath.
We pluck them, blue and
cloud-frosted as earth in space,
and hear their *doonk, doonk* in our pails,
we feel we've saved the relucent sea,
wind pressing garments to our flesh,
the present moment in a grail
for longer than it lasts.
Then when folded into batters or
stowed in a crust,
they burst their blue coronas
against a golden void, on our tongues
their sweetness runs straight through us
as if it were the blue blood of gods.

FIELD

In memory of George Bunker

It's not exactly the meadow
we've both looked out on
from different angles,
its grasses and berry bushes,
blue and bay, canted
to meet the sea, but the gist,
a realm apart from concrete existence,
yet derived from it, where,
from one of your big studio windows,
tethered to an oxygen tank,
you'd send your spirit out
to range and play
peekaboo, hide and seek,
in the clouded light
under a band of darkness
shining like mica.
Through many sketches in pastels,
you prepared a space:
quick, sparse, left-leaning strokes,
magenta, darker reseda patches
floating beneath a hazy green,
the wind blowing powder blue – all
give the effect of movement and depth
where you still reside,
inviting an elemental view.

A STAND OF SPRUCES

Behind my house, across a field,
spruces of varying heights
all raise their branches –
a conductor poised before a symphony,
a Greek dancer, a triumphant gymnast,
a child saying, Pick me up. Hold me,
a priest at the invitation to the Mass.
I want to paint them in brushstroke steps
that walk me into their stance,
but find the evergreen etched on my inner plate
portrays the branches in a down-slant.
It comes naturally for me to paint them that way,
downswept and black as the feathers
of folded crow wings. Nevertheless,
their uplifted limbs beckon like friends,
like kin already gone over, open arms
waiting at the end of the passage.
Drinking up earth, swooshing it
through their cambium,
has made them figures of trust, has
raised their arms toward heaven,
not knowing what it is, willing,
wanting to be shown.

FOR RACHEL FIELD

Sister soul, whose red-gold curls
and hazel eyes smiled gay
as Christmas candles,
whose heart was broken by
the alderberries' color,
for whom the swash of rain
on leaves, on sea
was lovely, liquidy miracle
and in whom rough, russet mums
struck fierce and secret fires,
you walked and loved these shores
before me. Before I was born,
you died too soon, singing these
trees and tides as I do,
these island ways and neighbors.
But unrepressed, your zestful,
elfin spirit bounds ahead of me
through gloomy spruce woods to
the russula, tunes me to its
bright bell's yellow,
the pitch of rapture.
Your voice in me resounds.
Older now by a year
than you ever were,
I pick up the melody,
the tone, fervent, exultant,
keep it going like a round,
shift the rhythm, alter words.

I want to chant it
pure and clear enough
to penetrate the ground you're under,
so your bones wake
as you prayed they would
to the music of this place
where far hills loom
over trooping firs and larkspur
blooming seaward, where waves
throw themselves down crying
and go out in pebbly laughter,
and the windows shine like friendly eyes.

ISLAND LIGHTS

On an island, it's consoling
to walk down the silent darkness
with wind smoothing hair
back away from your face
and pass the golden panes
of your neighbors studding
the path with topaz lights.
Out here you can get to thinking
you're alone, exposed as you are
to the elements, to infinity, until
in those luminous frames
you glimpse them, whose names
and ways you've come to know
bending over a book, a sink,
a mandolin, crossing a room,
ascending – all of them
keeping the vigil with you
together on the rim,
sending shafts out across lawns
into the blackness for a semaphore,
a signaling candle from beyond
this brooch of clear-cut gems,
polished bright with expectancy,
pinned to the bosom of night.

RED DOOR

Try painting a door red,
bright, true
red
in your white clapboard neighborhood,
just one door, that was
harbor grey
like all the others,
and watch
the reactions of neighbors.
You'll be surprised
that those you thought most liberal
are offended,
want it changed back
or suggest that
at least
you mix it with brown and dull it to
brick,
even when
you point out
a precedent
in medieval cathedral portals.
Others insist on
symmetry
and want all your doors to match it,
arguing that you can't have   just one.
It sticks out!
The uptight are
taken aback,
at first,
but admit, after awhile, that
it's grown on them and they
grin
when they cycle by
in spite of themselves.
The artist, of course, is

thrilled
and shouts   Hallelujah!
out loud,
but so,
believe it or not, does
the political conservative, who,
after all,
has a '48 Plymouth
he's painted brighter green than a   frog,
though you weren't sure
he'd think   you
had a right to flamboyance too.
But those you'd expect to support you
because of their own
flair and dash
hesitate
when asked how they like it
and say it's "lovely"
in very lukewarm tones,   and
when come the ones
you rub your hands together
hoping to   shock,
they don't even   *notice!*
No outraged comments
about its unseemliness,
its scandal.
What a letdown!
Because through it
you step forward unabashed
to divulge
your particular essence
to the world,
a cry — a whoop
a strut
a smooch, a sudden swatch of pure
élan vital.

ISLAND LIBRARY

In one room 20 x 30 a compendium of the globe
beyond this pocket of God's, edged with seafoam
tatting: *Women of Maine* pore over *Rosa Parks, My Story*,
Li Po and volumes to unveil our wonders, such as *Woody
Plants of Sphagnum Bogs* and *The Nocturnal World
of the Lobster.* Novels must be hot to drive off chills
or give them to distract from unremitting wind
lowing through high, uncurtained windows designed to let in
light shadowed with shaken conifers. Circling the shelves
are paintings, famous to amateur, diverse angles delving
for *The* Scape of our curled-up-with-a-book-shaped isle. Only
one name or initials needed to check out: J. G., Shorey,
Hans. By what we read we can be read: how often, how much
and more – between these covers, who has gone before us.

STORE

Cells from which the nuclei have been removed may live for awhile, but they do not function normally.
— *Encyclopedia Americana*

It's the hub.
The place to rub elbows with
those you might not otherwise.
Grubbies to uppercrust.
Sometimes hard to distinguish.
Everyone needs teepee eventually.
It's where to hobnob.
There's a hubbub.
Some hug, catch up, munching
tender, ferried-over donuts.
Others dilly-dally on the deck
in white acrylic club chairs
to contemplate the Bubbles
or chew the cud with Tud
and his Aussie sheepdog, Patsy,
over a cup of fresh-ground
hazelnut vanilla.
Some claim that aroma's the draw,
others the buzz or that here's
the only place near
to get the stuff
to get a buzz on.
It might be the foccacia, the arugula
fresh from an island oven or garden;
at quiet times, just
the refrigerator hum,
or the scuttlebutt: who scuffled
with whom
over the African mask
at the White Elephant Table,
what land is for sale
and why, whose

sails need trimming, whether
or when a hurricane's coming.
It's a vantage from which to watch
crazy kids cannon
into 50-degree "habbah wahtah."
On Tuesdays pick up your
Fish List special order.
On Freight Day at last
the milk they'd been out of.
Pay an up-front amount,
no wallet needed for a month.
They know you at the counter,
pull out your account
from which they can tell a lot.
Too bad the crack young woman manager
whose lamp you can see burning
after midnight over the books
is splitting from her ferry owner husband.
Islands are to marriages
as gale force winds to
launches left on moorings.
If no one else will take it,
and no one's come along,
it will close.
They say that if a store folds
and the school, which is down now
to two – and they're brothers –
so goes the year-round population.
Turn of the last century,
300 Maine islands
had native villages,
now only 11.

IDYLLIC

"TV ruined this island."
—Arthur Bunker

Out here men go out of their gourds.
They roar up and down a two-mile strip
gunning their pickups, wielding
tire irons at each other, shooting off
more than their mouths, their faces
red as lobsters dropped into the boil.
The off-island world spits on the dignity
their grandparents built planing hulls
and varnishing gunnels of
small craft in which every day,
no matter how many feet the seas,
how many knots the gusts,
they bait and pull up traps,
stack them empty on the docks.

BLACK-THROATED GREEN WARBLER
IN HONEYSUCKLE

So much smaller than you look in the bird book,
so much closer than you'd ever come
if there weren't this glass between us,
you frizz your bright yellow fuzz
right in front of me, pick tidbits
from these spidery crimson blooms.
You present yourself, reveal your
smooth olive back, black neck and breast
giving me a close-up, high resolution.
Are you trusting me, tiny sun?
My kind hacks up your habitat
for our Lebensraum,
drives you toward horizon.
Unwitting, you flash freely.
You relax under my ravening gaze
like Susanna bathing before the elders.

COBWEBS

Strewn across lawns like flyers
evangelical for the natural world,
they're always there, but not
visible until fog
strings their every filament with
Lilliputian pearls.
Sunny mornings we unknowingly
put our foot in them,
mow them down. Ten days of
thick mist and we finally
notice. Denied vistas, our
focus goes closer in and down
to these fairy nests, prairie towns,
feathers from the Great White Bird
grounded, gossamer, festoons, crosshatch,
coin catchers – larger droplets on them
are quicksilver doubloons.

They're springy. When we touch,
a dun-striped grass spider,
poised down a finely-threaded
funnel in the center,
scrambles up, legs tuned to
the twitch of an ant, tangled.
From her spinnerets she
secretes the silk she needs to survive.
Where does it come from?
How does she know to drape it
on these green rapiers?
We're snared by
the intricate mysteries
this concealing vapor has revealed,
our confinement in it, if only
momentarily, dispelled.

PERSPECTIVES ON FOG

for O and T

When you're in it, everything around you
disappears. Your mind too is clouded,
and you doubt the existence of shore,
of a road ahead of you, the nose on your face.
Is the world just a figment
conjured to console you and you
an island adrift? You feel as if
you're suffocating in cotton,
the materialization of your own breath,
and don't know – if the lid is ever lifted
and this stuff's pulled away –
whether what's left will be a stinking remnant
     or a gift.
                But this morning you're
on the mountain above it and, as it recedes
from the islands, you can see it envelop them
as nothing but
           chrysalis, a cleansing billow,
a pillow to blunt the points of the spruces,
a shell at last open a crack, a net catching
sustenance, tissue, caresses. A boat
sails in and out of it like a pilgrim
bathing in a mystic element. From here,
its purpose seems purely beneficent.

WRECKAGE

On an island at sea
in the woods,
in the middle of the woods,
Willie tried
umpteen times
to raise a house.
He'd lay out a plot
on spongy ground.
He'd frame it up –
vaults praying heaven
to hold him,
to keep him from himself.
Then he'd go on a drunk,
drive another truck into bog
where limp flags of wool grass
now push up through
the gutted engine block.

A windfall spruce would crush
what he'd manage to construct
or just when he got a roof up,
it would buckle
under heavy snow.
He ran through liquor and cash
like a whaler cutting wave ruts.
Beaten, broke, he tore off island,
leaving a heap of silvering boards,
windows tilted skyward, some
still in their frames gleaming
like panes of a monstrance, shattered.
Where he is nobody's sure.

It's hard to accept
that a life could
get so decimated:
insulation grown into the ground
like weird, pinkish moss;
mattresses coming unstuffed in underbrush;
a clothesline that saplings underneath
have grown tall enough to touch;
oil drums, engines and engine parts
transubstantiated with rust.

Why couldn't he ever get it together?
some ask, applying a second white coat
to Main Road clapboards, just
a market crash, divorce or
layoff away from
being lost ourselves.
If we never "make it,"
is there not something still
worthy in the attempt,
something stirring in a clearing
like this, silent as a chancel,
among our relics
a perfect shambles?

BLUE EGGS

for Gaile Colby

What did she want?
She'd never thought
and nobody'd ever asked her.
Never time enough, nor the means.
But with the kids, five of them,
finally gone, her mother,
after years of care, in a nursing home,
she thought, well, just for the fun of it,
she'd get herself some stock,
spend some of what
she'd manage to put by
caretaking for bluebloods.

It started with goats her stepson sold her.
African pygmies, cunnin' little critters,
blatting and butting each other, their hides
such fine combinations of black/white/grey,
it'd turn Calvin or DK green.
Romp and stomp. Nuzzle, nibble: spruce tips,
the special treat just beyond reach of
the pen she rigged up, with its hillock
made from old cable spools.
Does she breed them just to watch them
goof and gambol, just
to have some more to name?
There's Stanley and Teddy and Ethel
and Lucy Snowflake born in a blizzard.
Some with wetlets jiggling from jowls.

So many, she had a friend build her
a little barn, for them and the pig
who got too big for the house,
started moving furniture around.
Fancy just gets fatter and fatter

on gone-by soda crackers the store
sends down, 900 ornery pounds
that will never go to slaughter.

Only the hens earn their keep,
and just barely. Over 30,
and every oddball breed.
She peruses catalogues,
collects them like a set of live figurines,
one or two of each: pert Pedora Silvers,
Polish Buffs, Buff Orfingtons with
fluffy beige bonnets and feathery
bell bottoms. Black and white silkies
who "dust" to get that elegant sheen.
Reds, Leghorns, Bard Rocks,
sporting houndstooth suits, Japanese
Bantams in coats of lacquered rosewood.

Of course there are cocks, but only two.
The hens killed the others off.
There's Jigs the "squizix" roller pigeon
who knocks off gawkers' hats
zipping in and out of the barn.
People come from all around now
to see her island farm.

She can't get enough. Plans another
perch in the loft, a wing for geese.
Maybe to cancel years of want.
Bare cupboards and worn, unvarnished floors.
She's made propagation her art,
gets a kick at how the eggs just keep
appearing, every day more,
all sizes, some speckled, some
the palest powder blue. A delicacy
she sells to ladies who take them
soft-boiled with tea on ocean view terraces
exclaiming over the yolk's exquisite taste.

TRUMPET

Retired now, his heart blown open from attack,
the professor takes up again his horn.
I hear him playing every afternoon, two doors down.
He tries the notes at first like stones along the shore,
wobbling on some, losing his footing.
Nothing if not dogged from years of
searching, legs crossed, slouched,
through his cave of tomes for the needed fact
to confirm as certain his cherished theorems,
he presses on until he saunters, young
soldier again through Central Park,
hands in pockets, eyes up, awestruck,
the ring of towers, the radiant image of
a vanished woman: "Close as Pages in a Book."
That wished-for tune emerges, escapes, smooth,
debonair. He's become a jaunty Gabriel,
his music making love to the blue.

GEORGIE

No, there's nothing more important to her
than watching from her bed the sun ascend
over the strand at Schoodic,
than catching the balsamic moon
as it sets, close to her copious bosom.
No, the twittery fluttering sparrows
splashing in her bird bath
could absorb her a whole afternoon.
She always knows where the tide is,
when it will be low, and sits for hours
on the ledge in her cove to let
the waves wash her pains out:
her daughter's plane crash death.
No, she grieves the island ways,
the old ones gone: Hilda, Margie, Phip,
Ladies' Aid card parties, stitch sessions,
skits, making their own fun. Dances that
made the school's upper floor bounce.
No, women wore starched aprons then,
always chowder bubbling on the stove,
gingerbread in the oven. The men "yarnin'"
at Elijah's store, cat snoozing in the fish scale.
No, it's a shame to see the trash that
washes up on shore now: beer cans, condoms.
Day sailors trespass. Tromp without asking.
No, but she keeps fresh cookies on hand for
neighbor children. They keep coming
for them, for her hugs and interest,
even for her admonitions, the kindly,
shining turquoise eyes set in the
plain of her face, scored and weathered.
No, in her studio on the isthmus,
she forges stained glass tributes.
In wavery panes you can see the wind
lifting tufts on gull's backs, billowing

spinnakers, proud of their particular colors.
No, every place needs a guardian spirit
who worries and prays for its welfare,
who attends to its wonders with reverence
and she is ours.

GARDEN

Lay out a plot, a page
Soften the sod,
two years under cover.
Brood over it.
Compost extraneous
brain waves.
Wait. Wait.
The curing stage.
Fence it against raiders
varmints.
Lay it open and turn it,
turn it over with a
tiller till it gives
like well-kneaded clay.
Sore-shouldered,
stop, then pace.
Mull
what, where, when
to place.
Chop clods with
a cultivator's claw.
Ah-*yah*!
Make the soil fine.
Fold in exquisite
excreta
the slough from all
you've divined.
Rake it smooth and
level, a blank,
a blank brown sheet.
Hoe lines across,
shallow troughs for
sprinkling in seeds.

A chance
to write your name
in plants, to exhibit
grit, esprit.
Tuck and tamp.
Water and wait.
Mulch, water, wait.
Let them bake:
nuggets, rods,
pinpoints, comets.
With luck,
they'll swell.
They'll pop
and sprout sudden
tendrilous thoughts
struggling to develop
stems and leaves –
drafts scrawled
all over your patch
in fresh green script.
With thinning and weeding,
aerating,
they grow
out of themselves,
beyond.
They riot.
They flesh into petal
vegetable: lettuce, squash,
zinnias, cornflowers, limas.
Free within form,
fluent, eloquent –
a meta-language
that feeds and delights.

SLUG

Startled,
you bend down to look at it.
Alarmingly long,
it's fat, leathern,
and dull, ochery gold as
a very large pod of kelp –
that moves – but how?
Very slowly
this naked, unashamed
snail feels
with its long slick belly
every grain of dirt or gravel,
every leaf,
all its veins and scales.
Think of the silken caresses
it gets from the grass
all down its underself.
It's like a queen,
Queen of the Earth in
coronation robes with
a leopard-skin collar,
a tiger-skin train.
Eyes propped on the tips of
a two-pronged crown
act as periscopes,
provide her as she glides
with built-in perspective.
This long look has taken
less than a minute,
but slipping through your mind
is an indelible silver trail.

RED SNAPDRAGONS

Swaying wraith-like next to your oxygen tank,
bandana a red ensign over your baldness,
you directed the planting of the garden:
where to place the lettuces and beans,
the flowers, how deep to bury each seed.
Once mean with a hoe, you sat painstakingly
inscribing row markers, then, prostrate
on the grass, propped on an elbow, slowly
weeded the border. Like a starving mother
out of Kollewitz, giving her infant suck,
you invested last ounces in growth
you would not live to harvest. In late October,
after all else had withered, your velvet
black-red snapdragons, proud, monarchic,
bore your standard into the dark and cold.
This year, some of them skipped the road
to rise in my front beds!
Still giving from the other side,
you made them mine.

In memory of Esther Rome

OCEAN

Going down to the shore,
down a path starred with St. Johnswort,
you doubt anyone in the universe
is aware or wants to be of
what you're carrying, though
you may have tried to speak of it.
You seat yourself on a rock.
The deep seems to keep coming toward you,
reaching out to you in your trouble.
This is not its purpose.
It is not moving forward at all,
only up and down like
a tethered rope, shaken.
Urged by wind,
its nature is simply to
fold whatever it finds on the rim
into foamy scallops.
Let it take your tribulations.
It can roll them smooth as popplestones,
and they will take their place
among a multitude.
Or, they can be pulled out away from you
and get swallowed in
the crashing vastness.
It never gets wedded to a form
and its sonic massage can knead
the worry out, restore
your native self. When you see
suffering, you will not
have to try so hard to help.
Others will be drawn through you
to steadfast fluctuations
palpitating with light.

EDNA'S STUDIO

It is very clean in here
and clear. Everything
at angles, crisp and
straight. The surfaces
are blank, white or
gray, except the door:
bound-for-glory yellow,
and only as much light
as when a tight dun
sheet conceals the sun.
In fact, all the high windows
are clouded or veiled.
She clears this place
to clear herself:
she sweeps up all
the breakage,
becomes silent as
a sanctum.
Dustless and still,
she waits.
From a shelf, a phalanx
of paint jars
fires the room
with color, disturbing
the quiet as grains do
to make a pearl.
And it comes.
First the crayon
rubbed on
mulberry paper
over a rock
she's picked from
the shore.

Then a wash of
orange-vermillion –
she's never
tried this before –
water over wax,
cutting and placing
a monstrous sphere
above a slim,
gold strip of land:
collage, the idea
of fire taking shape
in the mind of God,
the sun scarred with
earth marks,
burning through ozone,
too near, but
finally true,
a magnificent danger
she's sold all else for –
out of the shatters,
something whole.

WEAVER'S PROMISE

Letters on a hand-painted sign
inside the ferry to her tiny island
spelled "Heirloom Weavers."
Just its sound was soothing.
And I was in need of that.
My fabric was rent. Even with rest,
it would not mend.

I took the path to her threshold.
Inside, it was dry and light,
bare, blond boards,
loom by a big bay window.

On a rack were finished goods
in lovely heathered hues: shawls,
throws, tunics, but I was drawn to
a basket in the corner of yarns –
small balls of rose, mauve, plum,
turquoise, teal and twinings of
pink-burgundy, lavender-royal:
wool lamps warmly glowing.
I knelt and fondled them.
They seemed to calm me.
The weaver, sensing it,
wove me a parable:

> When I was a child sick
> with pneumonia, no one
> thought I would pull through.
> A family friend, a salesman,
> gave me a tin full of
> ribbons, buttons, rick-rack,
> pins with multicolored heads —
> notions, we used to call them.
> For a long time, I couldn't

do anything but open the box
and move them around.
It was good, though,
to know they were there,
just waiting – raw materials
I could make something with
if I got strong again.

I spun this yarn myself
from fleece my daughter
sends me. She raises sheep
down east a bit.
Dyed it too, all natural.
Last winter I sent some
to a friend's got cancer,
thought the colors would
do her good. Why don't you
just take them – amounts
too small for me to use.

I insisted on paying.
She gently refused,
putting them in clear plastic
tied with a mohair wisp –
a bag of soft jewels.

I keep those balls in my study.
I love just to look at them,
to "feel of" them, as she would say,
and think of the millions of tiny
crosses it takes to make cloth.

CORMORANTS

Antic in black they
throw back their heads,
point hooked beaks to the blue,
look this way and that,
their necks like crooks,
their eyes tiny goggled jewels.
Up and in they loop
down for a fish.
The water is flat.
Are they gone for good?
Twenty yards off
they pop up with
alewives in their gullets.
That's it for work!
Hang out on the rocks
with the other guys.
Hang wings out to dry –
their own clotheslines,
like clowns with turned-out
pockets or flashers
opening overcoats –
funny faux Draculas.
Hardly the devils
Milton made them,
nor Shakespeare's
rapacious Time—
bum raps, snap judgments
based solely on their color,
their prehistoric lines.
Get to know them.
Watch them jaggersaw
into flight.
Then deny they're
more like comic relief
for the deep with its

super-serious ruminations,
and note that, except in love,
when they belch or choke,
they're mum as the also
black-clad Chaplin.

RED PLUM

I've never tried one,
a fruit ignored,
forbidden until now
by fear of the
voluptuous
which this ripe sun
has burned away.
From the sack you packed,
you proffer into my palm
its cool surprise,
round, firm, weighty.
Finely made, it's
underpainted
Tuscan gold,
over that,
Valpolicella,
the skin stippled,
a firmament
nebulaed lavender-grey.
It's cheeked, smooth
yet nubbly
to the touch as
your rump
driving in love
on soft moss:
this picnic
by the crying,
blinding sea.
Flesh sucked
away from the pith
is tart, is wet
and sweet, sweet
as if this
were our only day.

JAN'S GARDEN

Summer in her Maine island yard is
a jubilee, a *feu de joie*.
Once a painter, she tossed aside her palette
for living colors and laid herself down
a rich, cultivated bed whose dark
draws seeds, so all that is hard
and small and shriveled can break out
of itself. She delights in all flowering,
from campanula's delicate clappers that
could ring prayer from you to
salvia's palaver lined with
fuchsian secrets and violacious lies.
Hers is the Mother's invitation: Come
into being. Here's a place for you. Take
root. Show your colors! Yet she
apologizes. It's not neat, not spare.
No. It brims. It overflows. Everything
it seems has been "poked in" and tried.

In a corner where the ground gives up
a restful blue bouquet, around lobelia, mounded
deep and light, pansies let a bucket in you
down to get what a well can give: a
complete quenching. No fear.
Loving and nurturing are inflorescent here and
most in her scabiosa that pins you
when you pass it, its shaggy gridelin nimbus
raising up a convex nest of tiny, silvery
eggs, so whatever wounds you have twinge with
mending. Later, outside the window where you
dine, she's planted the night and scented it
with nicotiana stars and artemesia feathers
illumined by the white-silver of the moon.

You're moved by the outpouring.
It's as if a crowd stood on a pier for you
or rose in wild ovation to its feet, and
you marvel that anyone could care enough
to pull out all these stops: Bee balm
salvos. Feverfew bursting its little white
hoorays. Delphinium exclaiming in
delft, sky and plum. Gooseneck blowouts.
Torches of verbascum with their woolly leaves
outstretched, upraised, and in the center,
higher than all else, a fountain of
parti-colored sweet peas sending streamers out
over hallelujah dahlias big as lion's heads
roaring flame orange, roaring gold.

SALLY'S OBOE

this morning
here in this small island
church whose polished pine
refracts and
greatens the sound –
in spite of her
fuss and sputter
about it being
too cold – condensation –
water clogging the stops
and whether the
arundo donox
(you can *never* tell,
it's always like
walking a tightrope)
will allow the notes
inside her through
its pores in
the form, color and
speed she feels –
it's at once, nevertheless,
a divining rod
vibrating with the source,
dowsing for it in us,
and a conduit
bearing without
hindrance the kind of
refreshment deeper
than that tapped
from wells.
Because, through absolute
submission to it,
her breath
is fused with the music
shaped by

the muscles of her mouth,
the instrument
plays itself,
sending out the
sweet, sad banners
of this Bach sarabande.
It interprets the altar
flowers, a gay, variegated
font, fresh
for not longer than
this hour;
it reads the heart –
neither will we keep
in the glassy blue air of
this August vessel,
but how splendid
now to be joined
and held together
in this song,
a bouquet fragrant
and winsome
she gives into
the hands of God.

COMPOSER

Before I knew him,
I walked down his lane
one night in agita
and from his house
becalming strains
wafted around me and above.
Bach. Sheep grazing safely.
I learned you could count on him
of an evening to be at his piano,
as you could on the shy, amiable
radiance of his smile,
his ruddy face and pate,
ringed with pale hirsute clouds,
the companionable grasp
down my forearm to the elbow,
paying me the compliment of trust.

He invited us to boot-tapping
hootenanny evenings, assembling friends
with mandolins, saxes, bongos, with
guitars – electric, acoustic. Musical styles
from Dylan to Yiddish to Hank Williams,
recorders to Cole Porter, blues, bluegrass,
spirituals. Aboard the Chattanooga
Choo Choo through ragtime, piping for Danny,
striking up Sousa. Then, if coaxed,
he'd offer his own sonata,
published under the pseudonym
Monica Wells.

Meandering despond, dissonant doldrums,
the tension of two melodies at odds.
Keyboard-cracking turbulence,
torment aching to resolve.
Exquisite excruciations: loads
laid down in notes, on staffs
strong enough to hold them.
For pain, a bounded pasture.
He'd turn on his bench to face us,
mouth in a Buddhic curl.

SABBATH

From across the street we witness
every week their preparations:
all day the rising loaf, the roast's
heavenly aroma.
At five the children disappear,
leaning their bikes against the porch,
without whines, without grumbles,
to scrub, to get dressed up.
Who's coming? Why the fuss?
The Queen! The Bride! Friday night,
and through their window, candles.

What an honor then,
after we become friends,
to be invited into this celebration,
this humble, gentle joy,
that centuries, the world's temptations,
its worst-ever evils
have not quelled, cannot stop.

Out the big picture window by the table,
the tide is driving in, laying
a carpet, a dusky blue pile.
The sky is streaked with grenadine,
high color,
a banner over us.
As the turning earth erases it,
we embrace the comfort of each other's
company: Shalom, Shabbat,
kisses, hugs,
even teens with grownups,
kids with each other.

Danny raises his steady plangent tenor
to praise the Maker of the Universe
for our lives, for the sanctuary of
these hallowed hours.
Everything tastes divine:
the scarlet runner beans,
the garden greens sheathed
in garlic oil,
 challah's lemony gold.
We're savoring time, wine
rolling down our throats.
We feel eternal.

We linger over apples
Nathan's pie has sanctified.
We take our camomile,
let its quiet flowers soothe
our weary muscles, minds.
The candles, whose light
Cindy gathered like sheaves for us
at kindling,
burn all the way down
as they must
and we drink deeply as
we can of this love
that comes wanting
in us a place to dwell.

for the Rome family

NIGHT VISION

A tribute to Emily Nelligan

She floats down the road at gloaming
showing a faint but certain smile.
Like rabbis at dusk who wait
for the third star's appearance
to determine Sabbath's end
or hold up blue and white threads till
their colors blend at nightfall,
she perches on the verge at twilight.
For her this is when holytide begins,
when the island is relieved of
the complications of color, deprived
of its consolations as well, and all
is simplified to black, gray and silver.
Then she crouches on the shore
on a stone pile with her charcoal,
conte crayon and pad staring
with eyes keen as a boreal owl's
straight into the forest.
In her sights the dark is porous.
She sees how little light it can hold back.
Where those with night blindness
would search and search but miss it,
she finds and indicates a path.
Along it spruces prickle.
Grass tassels quiver under a moonless sky.
She could have guided Gretel and Hansel,
anyone fleeing ovens or
enduring the soul's dark night.
How does such vision develop?
From an overdose of rhodopsin,
from years of unlighted confinement?
In her pictures black is lambent.
Even death, as her scenes suggest it,
could be a soft, enveloping bliss.

STAR PARTY

Down through the Heath by bike
with only the moon to illumine
the gravelly route we call "I-95."
But what a moon! The harvest one.
As I stood with a friend at dusk,
we saw it rise out of the eastern ocean.
We watched it clear the trees,
a luscious cosmic apricot,
now so big and bright every needle
on a feathery tendril of larch stands up.

Hosts of the island's most remote house
have invited the summer remnant
to view through telescope the sun's
eclipse of this magnificent sphere.
Most of us here eschew the tube
preferring other entertainments:
each other's company, music-making,
croquet. Tonight our divertissement
will be the sky. On an island
fewer human lights
compete with the firmament.
We hardly touch the food,
a generous board laid out.
There is so much to see.

We can almost mark
the eyelid's slow sideways closing,
an amber shade that does not
completely occlude the full familiar face,
its blemishes still visible underneath.

Right below it, Saturn
presents the gleaming nuptial rings.
Jupiter, setting with his shining attendants,

is so intense, even in the dimming ether,
his greatness is reflected in the water,
whose waves supply perpetual applause.

An expert among us prompts
we should rightly have red flashlights
so as not to compromise night vision.
He wants to find the M-31 galaxy
in Andromeda – seed pearls
in a monstrous trove.
I make out only a foggy smudge
and Hale-Bopp, a chip of icy fire
aimed straight at us.

Oh look! The Pleiades, their
swarming, radiant cloud,
crown of the evening.
We train our binoculars toward them.
While we were taking in these spectacles.
the summer triangle: Altair, Deneb, Vega,
has moved 40 degrees.
How we are speeding, spinning!
As if we'd drunk this night's
dark champagne, taken down into us
the stars, their effervescence.

MOONLIGHT BOATRIDE,
AFTER A BIRTHDAY DINNER,
END OF AUGUST

We head out of the harbor,
seven friends with silver
starting in our dark hair.
The air is smooth against our faces –
calid night cream, the gibbous moon
so bright, marine organisms
drift up from the floor, and
those of us not normally given to it
find metaphors: farther out,
the ocean's surface is *fish scales*;
where the moon has pooled,
minnows of light, corridors of it, then,
fields of luminous grain, and the unspoken –
covers with lovers moving under them.
As we speed up, "punching that baby"
full throttle, moon brushes water –
rapidly changing characters:
mountains, islands, stars, no clouds,
earth marrying heaven.
Captain cuts the engine.
We're the only boat on the bay.
Extended silence.
Then, one celebrant says this night
makes her believe in reincarnation.
Any one immersed in this – water
light has so aroused – would come out
new, would come out better.
The other says he believes in *flotation:*
lunacy, this many of us in a 16-foot dory
after the feast we just polished off!
Again, we rev up. The last stretch,
plankton sparking in our wake,
we flay the inky deep, for brief
plumes of phosphorescence.

KEEPING THE FEAST

The table laid for us by two dear older women friends
is bright with handwoven blue-green mats and
matching monogrammed napkins. In the center
are red-orange begonia blossoms, floral exclamations
floating in a hand-thrown pottery bowl.
We're served up crinkly garden greens, vinaigretted,
succulent sea morsels and popovers high and crisp as
golden toques that, when broken, become butter cradles.

At each end a grande dame, a Seven Sisters alumna.
One a queen dowager has maintained her sandy curls.
On her face, like a tree venerable with rings, she wears
a perpetually amused, but for a touch of melancholy,
smile, and sometimes dons an Aged to Perfection
sweatshirt she bought herself. She gives papers
to her club on how comedy is used to
relieve tragedy in *Hamlet* and the *Henrys*.

The other, a consummate bohemian hostess who
performs loaves and fishes magic with casual grace
on an almost daily basis, though it might be pita and pate,
has burnished bronze cheeks, smooth as the surface
of certain beach stones, and hair with the grayish-white
sheen of gulls diving and declaiming over the waves.
She plays piano with a consort every afternoon and
organizes revels, still has a part-time job.
They tease about which of them presides,
the one who owns this house or
the guest who made most of the meal.

They regale us with gossip revealing the name of
the "snake in the grass" who caused the latest local
breakup, and what a shame (and a nuisance) it was.
There is gentle, hopeful, speculation about whether
the island renegade will ever straighten up.

There is a tale about a "bargain" secondhand mower,
bought from a native, which ended up costing twice
as much as new. The instant it changed hands,
it needed a new blade, a new battery, a new
this, that and, too big to fit in the shed,
required construction of its own little house.

Out the broad picture window, water
laughs and winks at stolid navy blue mountains.
Setting sun lays a path on it blinding as
the Damascus road. A struggle to get
shades down over the window, to filter
the light, but not shut it out.

Conversation shifts like the blue breeze to
a stabbing subject: Bosnia. In this lulling idyll
I'd forgot. Forgot old women, tearful in babushkas
in whose faces trenches had been cut. Forgot
the raped Muslim wife locked away till
she bore her enemy's child, the proud, silent
man whose penis was shot off to make him talk.
The food goes sour in my mouth.

I have been taught to muffle my life.
How could I enjoy if others suffered?
Should we abnegate this pleasure
and trade it for sackcloth?
I look around the table: in each of our families
ravages we've survived: madness, suicide,
bankruptcy, murder, incest, and yes
genocide, the Armenian one.
Healing to the point of feasting
has been hard won for us all.
We should not stop.

Instead, let us make a place for them at the table.
The grieving mother, wives violated, emasculated men.
Lead them to it gently. Assure them

we are not numb as the media claims.
Their pain pumps through us;
we know something of it. Its images
invade our dreams. Urge them to sit down:
There is still a place for love.
Surround them with this merry ambience.
Introduce them to these sage doyennes, their hostesses,
and place before them ice cream salved
in fresh blueberry compote. Let the aroma of
fresh ground coffee pass under their nostrils
and join hands around the table to show
the fabric of civilization has not been irrevocably rent.

BOG FRITILLARY

On the road through the Heath of this
ocean-swaddled place where I come
to peel down and quicken, sporadically,
red moss spreads like an alarm and
sphagnum, green-starred at the surface,
sucks black spruce and cedar into its
black muck below. Their trunks
wizen and silver. Lichen beards them.
Ravens, croaking like the tortured,
overshadow silver-green tamarack feathers
with their black, wide wings and far off,
a buoy bell knells. There, on the rutted,
puddled path sinking in sponge, a butterfly
lights on a patch of gravel and spreads
to let me note the pattern of its marks:
black waves giving way at the tip to
dots against a flame-orange ground.
Visitant to me as Mary's Gabriel, its
wings wink and I feel noted too, and
known, clear and definitive as those dots.

Is an insect sentient or has my need to be seen
as indelible, distinct, so sensitized me
that a pair of flexing wings appear to nod?
Debauchery drove Brother Francis to strip and
then for him the whole dumb world loosened
its godly tongue. Perhaps it's this.
Age takes me slowly as the bog does all
down into its black bed. This year, surely
more than half gone now, I fear its pull.
As if it knew this, the fritillary,
waving before it goes, quick over the quiet,
passes like sanctifying hands over a ciborium,
and for an instant, oblivion seems a chrysalis
to wrap and free the fluttering fire that
bears in black the characteristic markings of my name.

LICHEN

The designer of this island has a decidedly Victorian bent.
Frustrated love will find an outlet. Desire denied
fuses two life forms: fungus, algae. Their union
produces endless ornament to use the passion up
and slow-burn whatever it seizes upon. Eventually,
everything under this filigree will be gone. In time,
no rock, no tree, no stretch of ground escapes embellishment,
shy of beaten paths. Reserved for private quarters,
holy outdoor boudoirs, shore or forest, are
roan foliose ruffles, splashy saffron rosettes,
pearl grey reliefs with minute studdings of red –
filet, fruity accents. What ornate, yet elegant paraments!
The detailing! The inventiveness!

To break up a plain rock face, damask drapes of black-brown
umbilicaria mamulata. Glades hung with swags of aureate
bryoria create a seductive ambience. How chic,
bare branches sheathed in lacey *hypogymnia*;
while feathery, silver tufts of *usnea* grace the crotches.
The floor, cushioned with *clodonia turgida*, its myriad
squishy fingers, invites massage. Stones embroidered with
petitpoints of *porpidia* and manifold, various rondelles
make sumptuous brocade throw pillows. Even undersides of
outcrop are highlighted with chartreuse blush. Nothing
in these *intime* precincts goes untouched. Nondescript
trunks come to the forefront couturiered in rippling
lobarian chitons or doilied, medallioned, diademed by
plasmata glauca, their bark ridges limned with
shimmering squamules. And in a corner,
masses of tatting enhance a magnitude of rot.

Naturally, all this fancywork is hypersensitive,
squeamish about any atmospheric indiscretion, and
its producer is a fugitive who nimbly eludes taxonomists.
Only a handful of experts worldwide has any notion of
the scope of this opus, and they are elated and astounded
every month to discover intricate elaborations which
defy everything previously understood. These
are the few who have been lured by this tracery
into the interior apartments to commune through raiment
with the resident and return, carrying little
paper bags of evidence, decorated with awe.

FUNGI

Imagine a lumberjack, a rock chopper
turned out like a Copacabana showgirl.
It's hard work
breaking down wood,
chewing up cellulose
to make dirt.
Why not be flamboyant about it?
Why not lift a ruffled skirt?
Look at those little rungs
fanned out on the bark of a fallen fir,
how the color spreads like a rainbow
from brown to rust to gold to
at the rim a thin bright yellow grin,
gilded fore edge, pages of the Earthbook.
To say nothing of the gills,
the fluted underparts,
pretty sexy, pretty classy,
classy as Shakespearean ruffs
and loaded with spores
to make more such
functional frills.

Whose idea was this
that decomposition is cool,
that when you assist in
the disintegration of rigid forms
you feed the life force
(a little CO_2 for the greenery),
you give off tangible, fanciful aureoles?
It's as if God went around
sticking Post-It-Note haloes
on rotting trunks to say:
Take a look at this.
This is *good.*

POPPLESTONES

Why are they so appealing, these
dark, enlarged, petrified
seafoam bubbles, especially
the smooth ovoid ones? Why
do all who come to this coast
want to roll in their palms
the heavy warmth they've
absorbed from the sun, want to
take them home and set them
on a bureau or a sill to pick up
at idle moments and just feel?
Is it because mile-thick ice
bore down on the granite they're
made of and cracked but couldn't
crush it? Do we admire how
the tide rolls and rattles and
ravishes them to a polish high as
spit-shined cordovan, as Chinese
porcelain with an oxblood glaze,
as the finish of a Chippendale
tabletop – the fine workmanship
of the waves? As cobble they
took without wearing the rumble
of Boston's wheels, as ballast
they stabilized many a vessel.
Maybe if we have one we'll be
one. Maybe they'll hold us down,
hold us in place, and we'll be
weighty, permanent, essential as
they are, our roughness rolled away
by the ages, our edges rounded off
to the zero of one of these
begin-again eggs.

FERRY

The Sea Queen is our lifeline
weaving island to the Main,
to doctors, paint and shoes,
to movies and cafes.
And back again,
the loom is strung:
she brings the mail and
bears new fridges on her roof, bags
of concrete, diapers, spuds and dung.
30 feet by ten, her cabin's tight.
We have to intertwine.
It's hard to hold a grudge for long
when one who shuns you
or you shun faces you or gets wedged
next to you for the 20- to 40-minute ride.
Who are you if even stones
cannot withstand the smoothing
influence of this tide?
Each ticket punches through
your concept of another neighbor.
By the time you reach the dock,
someone whose name you weren't
quite sure of might confide with tears
about her daughter's drunken lover,
or stoic, stare blankly past your ear,
then flash a belying glance
if you dare engage. Babies
reach in glee for dogs; dogs
sniff back and lick. A hiker gets up,
turns and slaps you with his backpack.
In storms, she is the Ark.
You're tossed and grab
the arm of someone's houseguest.
In fog, Wilfred could be
Captain Chiron. Each crossing

brings you closer, a shuttle
spooled with weft, to batten
the threads of this communal life
into such distinctive fabric,
a fustian waled with waves.

SUMMER SAUSAGE

As they leave, summer people pass it on,
pass it off, pass it over. Originally a gift
from an overstaying houseguest,
a thoughtless one for a Jewish host,
who, though non-practicing, turned up his nose.
He made of it a hostess gift to a gentile neighbor,
thought it might be quite a hit with its giftish wrap
and claim of an "Old World Milwaukee Tradition."
Unbeknownst to him, the price left on
didn't quite match the claim in grandness.
The receiver was trying her best to
cut down on fat, so drew back
when he handed it to her.   Besides
since she was recently divorced,
he widowed, it felt so blatantly sexual,
though that was never his intent.
There are times a sausage is just a sausage,
but it turned her off. She was stymied.
She couldn't take it to the next party,
to which her neighbor was also invited.
(On islands social circles are so tight.)
She put it in the fridge and forgot it
till she had to clean and close up for winter.
She tucked it in a bag with other remnants,
considering it quite a prize among carrots
on the verge of sliming and milk just short of sour,
for her friend down the lane who was staying longer.
Some friend, the giftee thought. Doesn't she
remember? I choked and almost died on a piece of
sausage just like that this last November!
When she left, she gave it to her caretaker,
who had no taste for that fancy, fandangled deli stuff.
Give him straight kielbasa or sweet Italian.
So he took it to the mainland of a Sunday,
a present for his mother. She was wise.

By now it looked so handled,
cloudy plastic, curling label. She knew
he hadn't got it for her special. Besides
if he really cared, he'd know there's too much
salt in food like that for her high blood pressure.
So she tore the wrapper and chucked it
on the compost where the gulls raised a
fabulous ruckus for a chance to peck at it and devour.

FAIRY HOUSES

Baker's Island

Low to the ground and close to the path
leading to Dancing Rocks, they're fashioned
from twigs and bark, moss, lichen and stones.
They even have chimneys and porches,
backyard wells with thimble pails, diminutive
woodpiles, little lounges in front – every comfort.
From here antic denizens track day tripper traffic,
shake down conking cones, raise roots
to stub a booted toe. Enough to banish Baker's
from any Eden-chaser's wish list. Yet unbeknownst
to those who aren't really looking when
they're looking down, the wee ones also have
benisons to bestow on the only family willing
to inhabit this island, to live in Creation
unshielded. No electricity. No plumbing.
Berries are profuse: rasp and blue and goose
and are cached where tourists will not tromp.
Lost socks blown weeks ago off the line
appear on the stoop neatly folded.
When supplies run low, one can of tuna
produces boundless casseroles, and long
nights, a single log will keep toes toasty.
Here the hardy, who take rain whalings,
ocean's foaming mouths, the everlasting
vastness of the sky, dementing silences exclusive
to outermost isles, are also so keen and gamesome
as to have made the numinous a home.

HOME

I plead a nativity of the heart
— *Charles Wadsworth*

They tell me since I wasn't born here
and neither were my forebears,
since I don't winter over
or live off the waves, since
my a's don't originate in my gullet
and my speech doesn't mimic
the tide's tonal rise and pull,
I can't claim this place as home.

My parents never owned.
Every two years we moved.
I never knew what to say
when asked where I was from
until I walked up from this town's dock,
to the top of the rise, this corner
where a just-born breeze
whistles through berry brush,
where guardian gulls
take up their posts on roof peaks,
and a congregation of clapboards
faces the cold, the infinite
dark blue-green, like crepe de chine,
lustrous and fluctuant.

I flew to it instinctively as warblers
who return every spring to branches
that foster breeding, protect their brood.
They extol their niches with song.
Though they can't stay all year,
do we say they don't belong?

There's a moment when the floating seed
attached to a wing by its floss

finally drops, catches into its ground,
a safe, a welcoming host composed
to promote its growth and fruition.
Fifteen years from first visit to owning,
the day we closed on our beloved
double gables, my roots
balled up for a lifetime
let down.

When I pass through the door,
its multi-colored stained glass border,
the faint aroma of stove gas greets me.
The Ingraham clock
chimes at the house's heart.
One room opens on another,
kitchen to dining room to study
with wavery panes framing a field of gold,
letting in benedicting sun.

We've made this place a temple,
set an antique amethyst bottle
labeled Bitters on the sill,
bought washed pink wicker
to perfect the living room circle,
painted door frames periwinkle blue.
Still there is always chipping and peeling,
mildew, leaks and rot to ensure
our worship includes
the work of renewal.

I climb to the second story.
The sound of children at their dice games
reverberates, a raucous choir
up the stairwell. I entreat time
to stop, stop while I delight in lilacs
nodding under the window,
the view over saltwater plains
all the way to Frenchboro, across

toward ancestral Scottish isles –
beyond. From this perch
I feel native to these climes as
herb Robert, name of my fathers,
cropping up red-stemmed,
sweet-scented, intensely pink,
but modest among the rocks.

GRIEF'S PROGRESS

after Munch's Evening (Melancholy: On the Beach)

When you finally find home,
it's safe, at last, to be sad –
though you'd rather snap out of it.
You know that the walls of this place
will hold you,
and you won't be left.
You can go out front
and sit on the shore.
It understands "gulf."
It understands loss and erosion.
Remember yourself as a child
racing from school to them with your trophies.
Their silence. Their turning away from you
to fight. At night, shivering in your bed –
their awful explosions,
merciless, relentless as a blitz.
Pour your tears into the ocean!
In time the sea heals everything,
swabbing and swabbing,
your glass heart ground
by the waves into sand,
a smooth glittering expanse
that lifts into the sky and calls you:
another shore whose cities of stars
invite you into their streets to dance.

HAVEN'S THORNS

. . . to dim the too bright shores . . .
— Rachel Field

Our island is a blossom floating in the blue.
The road cutting up through it is a stem.
To walk it is to climb from thorn to thorn.
We cannot know the rose, that holymost of blooms,
without some pain. Each place along the way contains it,
or it escapes into the yard: the huge homes
looming with abandoned wives, the one with
blankets nailed across the glass, a propped-up porch,
the next spruced up just to sell for the divorce.
Here, neighbors never speak for years, forgetting why;
one will build to block another's view for spite.
There, the grouch who shouts all hikers off his path,
the father loud and wretched from the bathroom
rants, You fucking kids! You goddamn bitch!
Backshore, a hundred beer cans found around a fire
lit defying prohibition in a drought. On a nearby cliff
a jilted lover with a dozer turns the trysting cabin
on its head. A procession of dressed-up friends
pass us grinning for a fete to which we're not invited
while heedless minibikes grind up the breeze, the silence.
And who was it ditched the young parents' brand-new
truck below the tide line to rust it for revenge?
By the time we reach the end, the top, we're
pricked awake. We no longer scorn our common bush,
rosa rugosa rubra, as not quite aligned with
template Paradise. We suck its sour fruit, its hips
and stay alive, accept magenta, as close to red as
we'll ever get. We pick up background noise
and hear it now as rote assuaging our shore.
Still bleeding we accept the gauze of fog, let it
protect us from the stars which will, when we are
ready, transfigure us with their fire.

LITTLE SHRINE

The Holy Land for us is here,
this purple island haloed with
sea shimmerings and misty streamers,
and when we are away, we have,
on memory's altar, the image
of this place encased within,
an animated diorama.
We visit it to view with adoration
the waves, their sounding blues,
their movements, their moods,
the sunset's scarlet edge pastelling
slowly. Those spumoni hues
carried over mountains by nubbled
clouds suggest textures rubbed
from shore rocks, openwork veils
torn by the wind to reveal, before dark,
a shaft of absolute gold. We've
forgotten if this vision stripped us
of resistance or we came to it
threshed to the sensible kernel,
the spot the uttermost comes closest.
Contact with this sanctum quickens. Then,
wherever we are: in mud flats, waste or sprawl,
trapped in concrete canyons, cross, lost,
that land is consecrated too.

PUSHING OFF

Why do we cry at summer's end
and so hard, when
lines unhitch from pilings,
fenders flip up
and we push off from the dock,
our clutch of friends
waving and waving
broadly and long
till the gap expands and
we're swallowed in fog
or by horizon?
We've had such fun:
Firemen's Suppers,
the Ladies' Aid Fair,
Wimbleberry, Tangleberry,
birthday cruises up Somes,
picnic hikes to Crow and Sutton,
back and forth borrowings,
cinnamon, butter,
talks on porches, tea over Scrabble,
quiet candles,
and such prodigious laughter.
Shouldn't we be cheering?
We'll see everyone next summer.
But no, each year
diminishes our number:
Jeanne, Bob, Keith, George, Esther.
One less irreplaceable face
to greet our return, should
we make it back ourselves.
Too many silent tributes out there,
the mail boat under us
creaking and rocking,
as, after their ashes,
we cast our garlands,
colored crowns.

TOWARD GREAT CRANBERRY
ISLAND, DUSK

Behind mountains that have stood
since Abnakis lit their fires, since
glaciers pulled back a frozen veil
upon them, their contours lying
like the waiting body of a woman,
the sun goes out carnelian,
the color of coals, the color of
ingots. Like our time here it melts
into the ocean, marbling it aqua,
vermilion, its fire holding
only a little while against the water.
Beside me our daughter curls,
a periwinkle, her head in my lap.
Under us the engine hammers,
getting us out away from the shore
to this island, this spruce-spired
glade, shored up with rocks,
its tabernacles, its incense.
Under gables that will hold longer
than we will, our bodies build
a fire against the chill of night.
Our minds flame with words:
cove, shell, swell, points, buoy.
We are a conflagration, only
bone fragments left to be sucked
and swung, thrown up on some
other shore, detritus,
found and fondled, thumbed
in pocket, kept.

DEDICATIONS

Lobelia – for Margaret Cox

Tea Ceremony, Under Apple Tree, August – for Martha Rome

Wreckage – with thanks to Dorothy Silvers

Blue Eggs – with thanks to Arvard Savage

Trumpet – for Dick Cox

Georgie – for Georgie Ware

Edna's Studio – for Edna Andrade

Jan's Garden – for Jan Moss

Sally's Oboe – for Sally Bloom

Composer – for Bill Goldberg

Star Party – for Dick and Kitty Pierson

Moonlight Boatride, After a Birthday Dinner, End of August
    – for Ann and Dick Sullivan

Keeping the Feast – for Betty Hartley and Gina Murray

Lichen – for Abi Rome

Little Shrine – for Edna Andrade and Betsy Wells

Toward Great Cranberry Island, Dusk – for Gina Murray

ABOUT THE AUTHOR

Susan Deborah King teaches creative writing and leads retreats in Minneapolis on creativity for personal and communal growth. Earlier in her life she was a Presbyterian minister and psychotherapist. In the summer she lives on Great Cranberry Island, Maine. She lives with her husband, James Gertmenian, and is mother to grown twin daughters, Emily and Enid.